letting go is how i love you now copyright © 2021, written and performed by Tiffany Aliyah Davis.

All rights reserved. No part of this book may be reproduced, performed, or used in any manner without written permission of the copyright owner except in the case of reprints in the context of reviews.

www.tiffanyaliyah.com

to all the boys i loved before. . .

letting go is how i love you now

love...8

loss..46

letting go..80

*me, you, us, past lovers, my inner child, love, God

i'm coming back up from under the weight of you
the way we slammed into each other felt soft until i landed
until you toppled over me and i toppled over you
and got crushed in the heaviness
i've spent the last year buried here
buried with the ghost of you next to me
who i don't recognize, but still can't look away from
i carved you there, cradled in the bones of us
with one hand on your heart and one hand digging for my own pieces
hoping i still saved enough healing for me

i'm coming back from that. i left what remained of us there.
i washed it clean with my tears and planted flowers with you
the energy of us will bloom into something beautiful again
for someone else, in another way
but today, i unearth myself from the depths of what we were
i send you love, i wish you peace, and let you go.
i crawl myself away, with everything new i gained
into what was always mines to grab a hold to
with new seeds, standing between the light, back into the warmth of loving me
again.

letting go is how i love you now.

letting go is how i love you now

what has your experience with love been like?

letting go is how i love you now

love

(in all forms and variations, in the falling and then colliding, in all the heaven and the hell of it, in all the lonely and joy it brings)

a letter to my ex (who was never really my ex)

you weren't always toxic
the gentleness in your voice when you called me beautiful sung satisfaction into my soul
knowing that you were proud of me tasted like cocoa and açai
it was sweet, and warm,
gratifying.

i woke up this morning with your scent in my sheets
the taste of your tongue on my lips
the imprint of your rough hands bruised my hips

   i forgot what missing you feels like

you weren't always toxic
on my eighteenth birthday, you wrote me a thirteen-page text message with all the reasons i shouldn't feel insecure
i called you crying, and you stayed on the line with me until i fell asleep
at times, you had a softness to you that evened out the ugly in me
a voice that spoon-fed complacency into my gut
it took me a while to see you were maybe a monster

   i thought you were a God.
   you were adonis and i loved you.

   many loved you.

i try to remember that, in these moments of nostalgia.
in the moments when missing you crawls down my throat, creeping into my bloodstream and alienating all the reasons that i hate you

it's been a year since we last spoke.

it's getting harder to hate you.

sometimes it's really easy to hate you.
   but you weren't always toxic.
   and as much as i try to forget
   i can't erase all the moments where you played superman to my lois

i can't erase the moments you made me feel like gold.

letting go is how i love you now

chasing sunrise

i miss the feel of your lips in between my shoulder blades
in the early morning hues of virginia skies
in the pinks and amber shadows of when you thought i was asleep

i hardly ever slept

not because i couldn't
in truth, your arms were enough security to calm me asleep for a lifetime
you were my blanket
but staying awake slowed down the moments when i was away from you

i always knew we were temporary
but there was something about the shadows of 6am that felt like forever
i wanted to memorize everything about you
your snore
your scent
the position you slept in when we weren't tangled together…

i miss you.
i think i'll miss you forever.
i'm still yours
even if i am not yours

sunrises still remind me of you

dear ____:

i am already creating scenarios
of what it will be like

to see you again...

fragments

ask me about our first kiss
and i'll sing you melodies of intoxication
ask me about the time you called me beautiful
and i'll shine star bright fireflies into your chest
pound heart beats into your palms
until your hands become pedestals again
until my lungs shatter from holding fistfuls of i miss you' on my breath
and smothering flames of spirit inside my throat

ask me why i loved you

and i'll let our memories slip off my tongue until we're drowning again
after months and months of ignoring flashes of happiness and heartbreak,
there are film strips of images and time and us that dance against my mind,
with fragments that were never strong enough to build a foundation
but potent enough to keep my love for you living and breathing between
the silence of us being over
as much as i told myself to forget
the ringing of your name whispers in my loneliness
nostalgic rhythms play our fragments in drum beats that pound
consumption
until, eventually
enveloped in your memory,
i surrender.

kissing sand

every time we touch
i'm left with something new to remember
something new to hold on to
another moment not to forget

                        the feelings
                the sounds of our voices
spiraling within the silhouettes of how we move
                         how we come
                how we breathe together

                        we move like a lingering song
                to words you don't want to stop hearing
                    and a voice that hums like love
                      with a swiftness of a shooting star
                      with the calm of a full moon
blending our rhythms with intimacy and salty scented sweat
                            our hips are the bases
                      and our moans are the ad libs
                            always in tune,
                          always harmonious,
                            always beautiful.

letting go is how i love you now

atlanta

sometimes (or all the time), we want our happiness to be long lasting, and not just temporary paradises we have to leave behind someday soon. i feel like i've lived most of my life having all these separate, epic moments of ecstasy filled joy. and then, like a falling star, it's gone. as fast as it appeared. people ask me (i even ask myself), "why do you keep doing this? why keep taking these leaps into briefness for temporary fulfilment?" the truth is, i don't know how to exist in any other way. i don't know what a constant happy is. i don't know how to hold onto it. i don't even know if it's real.

so i jump.

i jump and i leap and i dive into these fleeting joys, drinking in its elixir like it's my last sip of water until i am overwhelmed with the idea that

this could be forever…

and sometimes it's simple.

it's pebbles beneath my toes in riverbeds that flow against the creases in my skin. it's looking at my body against yellow glows, feeling the sweat building underneath my armpits from hard work. it's the sound of morning sunrises and the way the earth is so much greener in other places. it's in the way that i bend, and twist, and dance myself into thoughtlessness until i am dizzy and in love with myself again…

and sometimes it's complex

it's moaning against skin that i've only ever dreamed of touching. it's being called baby. having my door opened for me. listening to snores that aren't my own in the quiet hours of comforting darkness. it's being kissed awake, or

kissing awake, the type of man that i imagine loving me one day.

it's pretending that i don't want more, to get through the night…

it's knowing that i don't need more, to come back to reality.

it's giving up the idea of constant,

just so i can get through to tomorrow.

letting go is how i love you now

nostalgic

                        i wonder if you knew what you were doing last night
               if you purposely branded your touch on the inside of my skin
                  polished your breath against the whispers of my heartbeat
                         just so i could hear the echoes of your pulse
                               shout nostalgia against my mind
                          on nights where my body heat radiates cold
                                         and loneliness

         i wonder if you purposely hid a small piece of yourself inside of me
                                 so i wouldn't forget you
                              if you only called me gorgeous
                                    just so i'd remember.

after work

*i am not accustomed to my hands being wrapped in someone else's palms
so, forgive me if i stutter every time our fingers touch...*

hardly whole

i want nothing more than to lick your wounds
and fill the spaces between our emptiness with my love for you
i wish i had the power to fix you.
to make you feel as whole as i did the first night we made love
but i think that's the problem.
you ~~complete~~ me on a level you have never earned
and forcing you between the spaces of my loneliness and insecurities
has left me broken.

love prayer

if you could see you in my eyes
if i could see me in yours
we could heal and move through to glory
if we could grow in each other's glow
if we could flow within each other's path
we could heal and create in Gods glory

surrender to yourself, and i'll surrender to me
i'll dance in my shadows, while your music plays
it'll sound like your light in the shade of your trees
and we'll find breath in moonlit forests

surrender to you

as i do to me

surrender to Love

surrender to you

i'll surrender to me

we surrender to God

we surrender to Us

letting go is how i love you now

dear _____:

it would be easier to let you go.
as hard as it'd hurt
as tantrum as i'd become
kicking and screaming and gargling your name between raspy
breaths of already missing you across the threshold of our back
door...

it would still be easier to leave
than to stay and break anyway

whoever said that loving someone was easy?

it is not fair
that every emotion i own
has been invested in a bed of love
unrequited
unreturned
and every night
i drift off restlessly
wondering why i've put so much hope
into a dream you're so ambivalent towards
maybe i am asking for far too much
dredging these fantasies that scream
you and me
it's 4am
and i'm tired of craving the reassurance of your name on my phone.

letting go is how i love you now

honesty hour:

i wish i knew how it felt to love without one hand on the trigger. sometimes i feel like i make romance stories out of tragedies. i still can't see the ending.

inconsistency

if there was any lesson that i had to learn the hard way

it would be that some people do not care if they lose you.

you walk around with welcome signs plastered on your forehead because loving has always been your closest comfort

you love to love

you're a kaleidoscope of questions and getting to know new people

butterflies are your best friends

you enjoy first times and romantic skype conversations

you're amazing.

and i feel bad for you.

because some people do not care if they lose you

and you don't deserve to be lost.

and i can see the lump in your throat growing larger from all the people who left you mid-sentence

all the words you never got to say

i know you're choking on yourself

and choking on the parts of you they left unsearched

i know how terrified you are of inconsistency

because it's almost always equivalent to loss

i know you don't want to smile right now.

i know you're not okay.

karmic ties

between deep breaths, i see the tickle of your fingers lingering within the interval of my shoulder blades

i feel your air on my neck and your palms on my back

my breath stumbles over the feel of your lips touching me,

frozen and warm

frozen and open

i smell the ocean breeze and lean deeper into you

and into us

                          i want to show you to the world

                let me dive into you, heart first and unabashedly naked

                                        you hold me

                              in ways i've never been held before

                                          skin to skin,

                                          legs entangled

    foreign tongues colliding and speaking in a language i forgot to remember until you

                                                      kissed me

we feel ancient

like a past life,

ritualistically bonded

familiar and still lingering between the ellipsis of now and then

between maybe and prophetic...

this is real

and this is raw

and this is everything i've ever wanted and more

you're everything i've ever wanted and more

hold on to me

dive into me

grab my hand without second guessing

and i promise i won't let go.

letting go is how i love you now

i fall apart faster than i can put myself together
is that what life's about?
sorting through the pieces of myself with four-week-old acrylic
tips from the last time i saw him—

you'd think it would get easier
that the next heartbreak would heal easier
that i'd be able to see clearer and move quicker
i'm six feet under and digging myself deeper
i've been here before and recognize nothing
i understanding nothing
nothing except that i fall in love faster than i could put myself
together
i never put myself together.

fireworks

he dazzles me.
like fireworks
i stare awe faced
open mouthed
entranced
eyes wide
afraid to blink just in case i miss the way his hair falls as he leans in to kiss me
i am mesmerized
mesmerized by all the ways his smile lights up my world
shocked by the way his laugh sends my heart into a chaotic pounding that reminds me of running barefoot

this may not last
but i stare awe faced with two hands on his heart;
he is a firework
and we look like the smoke and ashes that are left behind—

he dazzles me.

but—
fireworks fade.

and i become nostalgic for his hands way before the blues and greens have left our sky
i sometimes forget

i am the star.

burning bright and stripped raw
my light has been shining way before the fire from his kisses stunned me
into this alternate reality
as much as i hold on to him,
i must remember
that the best gift i can give me
is to keep one hand onto myself
to remember that my light contains fires big enough
to reach the hands of God

letting go is how i love you now

bright enough
to shine through the gates of heaven
i am a galaxy of beauty that distracts the most beautiful of sunsets

he may very well be a firework,

but my light will hold steady with or without him

i am more than flutters of beautiful.

i am more than the kid i become after seeing a fireworks show.

swimming lessons

i never learned how to swim

i've been obsessed with the ocean ever since i was a child

watching little mermaid movies and spending hours bathing in underwater castles and love stories

i'm fascinated with the way water meets sunlight

like energized crystal beams personalized for the aura around my heart

i feel most at peace to the crash of waves and the way everything sounds far away,

even when it's right next to you

i like how i feel when i'm underwater

even though i have trouble opening my eyes

it's like hearing whispers from the boy you like

from way across the room

your name on his voice and your heart on his mind

your scent on his skin, even if you can't touch him

even if you still can't reach him..

i don't know how to swim

and i'm not sure where to start

or how to learn without angst

as much as i love the ocean,

i'm afraid of falling in

i'm not sure if you should save me, when i don't know how to save myself

i don't know how to fall gracefully

and i know there's no real landing

letting go is how i love you now

i'm standing at the edge of my life
peeking over the diving board of my story
terrified of what it'll look like, or what it'll feel like once i jump
always fighting, always working, always searching for the next life raft to keep me afloat

i don't know if i should jump
i don't know if i have a choice
but to jump.

honesty hour:

it's a different kind of hurt to have so much to hold onto but still not enough to fight for.

letting go is how i love you now

speaking terms

there is a loud whisper
between the spaces of our fights
that lingers in the ellipsis of us not speaking
it says:

"you are better than this"

and i cringe because
well
the truth hurts.
and i am not quite ready
to let you go.

mirage [part 1]
- something that appears real but it's not

he's drifting through oceans with no idea of where shore is
he's swimming through hurricanes
and resting in sunsets
i was merely a pit stop
his island in a sea full of illusion
that housed all his insecurities
and loneliness
a small plot of land that offered him second chances he wasn't ready to take
i was a mirage
an image that faded before it could ever be painted
before he could gain the willpower and strength to claim me as his own
i fed him the fruits of my island
and washed his face in my tears
i let him lay down his kisses in the sandy grains of my heart
and rest under the sun in my love
i conjured first-aid kits out of tangled seaweed and bloodstains
and did my best to blow away his pain
but it was not enough
we were only a mirage
a romantic island get-away at the tip of his tongue
but no amount of words could keep him
or me, from reality
he's still lost at sea.

letting go is how i love you now

the things i told this boy i love, that i should have been telling myself:

i wish you could see the halo between the spaces of your smile.
i'm filled with light at the sight of you.

six seconds

for the next six seconds, i'll smother my face into your smell

hands held gentle across your chin

we breathe together and i hold on to you

and us

i pray i remember this.

when my triggers show their resentful face

i pray i remember us.

when my trauma exorcises its way through my thoughts and i trip over sanity

when my brain betrays and my resolve stutters across our cracks

i pray my heart is strong enough to beat steady

to remember what calm is like, and slow

to remember chin to chin and cheek to cheek with you and eyelashes flitting across my

face in love,

for love, i'll hold you tight tonight

for all the nights i couldn't and all the nights i can't and all the nights i miss,

for the night i can't forget

i'll kiss you right tonight,

like maybe it's our last

like maybe it's our future and we just don't know it yet.

when missing you feels heavy

i'll try to remember this

i'll love you right tonight,

for the moments where i forget, and the moments i regret,

i'll love your light tonight

letting go is how i love you now

and hold on to us in the darkness.

until the skies clear,

i'll hold you here.

rough

he was rough.
jagged edged and incomplete
like uneven breaths
words on the tips of tongues,
unfinished sentences and unsaid thoughts
kisses with questions and no answers
he was love and fleeting
i both loved and hated him for it.
he'd tell me he loved me in his restlessness
where only he could taste the honey on my tongue, the forgiveness on my breath
he'd rest those soft words on my chest when he missed the comfort of my exposure
and molt me to lava; into poems and kisses and smiles i only believed in when he was around.
and yet, i lay still as he skipped hot coals across my love
melting swiftly within the blurring of lines between lovers and friends
and the soft, smokey whispers of comfort left trickling across my flesh
as his fingers caressed longing beneath my skin
the sound of his presence lingered between the best of heart break songs

i made love to our memory
watched sunsets disappear on winter evenings
gently tracing the outlines of his hands against my back
rough, against my neck
choking and grasping for breath that would never come.

letting go is how i love you now

five years

all i've ever wanted from us
was to love you
without shame
to be loved in return
without hesitation
while you hold your tongue
between the empty spaces of my honesty
and close your eyes at the sight of my audacity
my bravery
i am still searching for ways to poetically admit
that five years of loving you, though it took courage,
may never be enough.

love, again

drifted into light

our light

your light

purposely observing the clasps of our hands

i say a prayer

and you baptize me in your palms

there's hope here

there's God in this

we feel real again

letting go is how i love you now

we can love again.

dear _____:

i didn't want to walk away from this
but choosing you meant losing more of me
as much as i love you
as much as i loved us ...
God said, 'love **Me** more.'

--i hope you understand...

letting go is how i love you now

what does grief look like for you?

letting go is how i love you now

loss

(to honoring the grief in all its agony that is birthed in the ending of a bond, to unraveling the ties that connect me to them, to mourning the beauty, acknowledging the un-beautiful and finally setting us* free)

mourning doves

they say our bodies keep the score

well, i carry the pain of us between my shoulder blades

struggling through the day to day to get to the quiet place where i can close my eyes and

finally ignore the whispers of you that scream out memories on every street curb i call

home

i do all this crawling through the mud of us

only to feel it later, aching alongside my spinal cord when i stop to rest or stop to

breathe or stop to think about anything other than surviving without you

i don't know how to let you go

at this point, it feels like we're tattooed beneath the tendons that hold my limbs together

it's hard to stand up straight

it's hard to move

it's hard to see past what tomorrow will bring when i still feel the weight of you digging

between my shoulder blades

i need you to let me go

i burnt your love notes and i deleted our pictures

i blocked your number and poured our ashes into the sewer drain

so why you still here

why does my back hurt

why can't i walk no more

every day i tell myself i'll start tomorrow
but morning and mourning comes and i still don't know the sun.
every corner i turn, i'm struck by the sight of us
in white square shaped SUVs and hilltop cafe
in the sound of the waves and the oils you bought for me

i smell you in the water i bathe in

you still lay beneath the surface of my prayers

we barebacked across every part of my core & i don't know how to wipe you clean
we aren't fading yet

is this grief?

will i feel the remnants of what we were & what we could've been, forever?
in the death of our forever, does the mourning have an ending?
does love have a death?
will missing you always be this heavy?

letting go is how i love you now

honesty hour:

how do people deal with grief in grace?
i don't feel graceful at all
most days i'm snotty nosed with tear cracked lips
with a mouth full of how could he's and how did we go so wrong
i don't know how to put us to rest
i wake up every day with our last breath still caught in my chest...

going rogue

it was like digging through trash piles.
cutting myself on blades of fear as i searched for the splintered pieces of my heart
lost in your insecurities and excuses
i gave you a piece of me
used but whole
and i asked you to take care of it
so how come i'm finding shards of myself in your empty words
and stumbling on crumbled love that you placed in your pocket?
how come i'm pulling blood clots out of your voice
and finding your fragrance in my veins?
you say you care about me,
so how come i'm finding every part of myself smothered in your apologies
swimming in your lost smiles
and suffocating in your broken promises;

my heart feels demolished.

how come my chest pumps
st-
      st-
            st
                  -stutter every time i hear your name?
i should not feel dazed from loving you.

        so how come?

i gave you a piece of me.
used, but whole
and i asked you to take care of it
so how come you used it whole and left me with a crime scene puzzle?
and now my visions too blurred from tears to figure out what goes where
i don't know how to recognize the difference between closure and security
or how to recognize the difference between comfort and stability
i'm too fucked up to remember the sincerity in my actions before you ever kissed me
and now i'm kissing n*ggas out of spite who really wanna be with me
i don't know if i have feelings or if i'm only prolonging myself from healing
by singing the same sob stories that convinced you

      you can't be whole anymore.

letting go is how i love you now

you put on black V-necks, flipped up your hoodie and called yourself a rogue
and now i'm painting my heart with shades of red lipstick because

        i don't want this hole anymore.

but it's only a coverup
no matter how many layers of red i smash into my skin
when i cry, it gets washed away
revealing these scars that won't fade away
i'm bleeding out into the landfills that you created
my mind is wrapped in strait jackets, i haven't been the same
and that hole expands past my heart, into the very core of myself that i've been trying to keep sane

        i miss being your island.

                but your tsunamis crashed into my chest
and i'm suffocating on your mistakes as i get washed away into your storms
                    if you haven't noticed by now,

        you fucked me up.

        but i guess it's just a part of that vicious cycle.
           you made a fool out of my love

        and now i'm just like you

you know, it was hard. this whole time with him was filled with so many ups, but so many downs. and then we finally crashed. and i haven't completely picked up the pieces of myself that broke in that crash. i'm still trying to find them in all our memories. and phone conversations. and kisses. and teach them how to be without him.

letting go is how i love you now

on film

there are silhouettes of you thumbtacked against my veins

attached to the spaces between my rib cage that refuse to forget you

some days they look like Polaroids

i breathe in the best of us & remember what it was like to love the hell out of someone

and be blinded by heaven

i let myself overflow with missing you until i forget we're gone

until i forget that heaven left us the moment you set your sins free

i don't know how to forgive you for ruining us.

most days we look like mugshots

stenciled into my subconscious until my dreams become nightmares

images that force me to accept the truth of our story

as beautiful as we were, your demons were far too greedy to just let you love me right

and we were ghosts the moment you decided to try anyway

i am reminded of the cracks you all left in me
i am splintered in places i can no longer see to repair

how will anyone love me like this?
how will i ever love myself?

crash landing

i feel like i lost my person
i never wanted to be just a lesson for you
God why couldn't you let us have this?
in all our pain and all our trauma, didn't we deserve each-other?
the best of each-other?
didn't we deserve this love?
haven't we been through enough?
was it all real?

it felt real.

it felt like light and forever
it felt like you get me and i get you and we in this together
i never wanted you to be just a lesson
i never wanted to look back on us and feel disconnected
i only wanted to look forward
to us, to you, to me
to new beginnings and new love and a new way to worship God
with my hand on your chest and your smile against my neck and your palms on the small of back,
i felt the safest i ever felt.
i felt seen
i felt...
felt.

i wish it would have been enough for you

i wish it were enough to still grasp onto

to hold and be still.

to love and be loved.

to move when you move.

to fall and land softly...

letting go is how i love you now

soul searching:

is being alone as ferocious as it seems
will it protect me from the things that breathe heartbreak?
is loneliness actually the hallelujah of it all?

lock and key

your kisses placed on my lips have turned into stamped fingertips for prison cells
your name on my tongue taste like guilty in murder trials
i'm lying on these witness stands to protect the image i believed i saw in us
but why does visiting memories have to feel like committing crimes

my fingers remember you
i can trace the curve of your spine and your adam's apple in my sleep
my palms search for you
even though i never had the warrant on your heart for permission to committing crimes,
these memories just won't listen to
me
or you

moments of past came here to find you
and now,
i'm suffocating on the pieces of me that stayed behind
they never knew that the rhythm to your voice could only ever mean goodbye, so they're still saying hello to remnants of kisses and dancing with fickle alibis and telling lies about what could have been
and what really happened.

the words what if are like my second language

but i can't convince myself i'm innocent with any of this
i let you back in
and now, i feel like i'm committing crimes every time i close my eyes, i guess i should start placing memorials on my heart
maybe then i'll stop stalking your shadows in movie theaters and stop trying to stop time in our phone conversations
maybe then i'll stop listening to the hum of your breath whispering

promises you never even made me

maybe then i'll stop tracing our silhouettes on thin paper because i promised myself i'd never write another poem about you

maybe then i'll stop committing crimes against myself

but here i am

and there you are.

locked in the flesh of my spine

still controlling whether i stand tall or remain weak

you're my jail keeper .

or savior

i don't know the difference

and though you have exit signs that throb louder than your pulse

i won't go

i can't.

we, us.

it was after cutting my fingers tips
on reflections from our past
and sweeping up the shattered glass left around my heart from us
that i slowly realized truth
on shaky and raspy breaths
we . . .
we were never meant to be
and hope,
can only be cracked
so many times
before its gone.

letting go is how i love you now

half whole, half broken

two broken halves don't make a whole

sitting on this creaky floor in the shadow of your light
this use to be safe

breathing feels like labor now
arms wrapped around my torso, holding all my insides in

you nurse your bruised knuckles against my chill
there's blood against the wall
we ain't ever felt this beaten

splinters underneath my feet now
they fell in your divulgence
i swept them together and they stuck to me

i can see the dirt under your fingernails
looking like graveyards
was it always there?

you fiddle with your hands
and avoid my eyes
your palms don't hold me now
my mind don't want you now

i look away

we sit in statues here

i shift and we crack

i cry and we freeze

you move and we shatter

we touch and it stings

we love and it hurts

we love and it mends

we love and it falters

we lock eyes and it's clear

two broken halves make more holes

two broken halves can't be whole.

ideation

i wish people could see my thoughts
to make sense of these
shattered vases
expanding canyons
quiet sips of passion left inside of me.
i'm the type of girl who dreams of her own funeral
of choked-up speeches, and tears
of tragic car accidents
broken spines contorted from the fuck ups and wishful thinking that left me
shredded,
scattered and shuffled like abandoned paper on the wind
i'm the type of girl who sits in solitude on concrete sidewalks,
head relinquished to the heavens
glistening eyes praying to the sunlight
scarred hands
legs extended to intersections
exposed
broken
. . . free,
and wonders what it's like to be remembered.

a story half told

it's not having access and knowing others do
i never had to quit on anyone until you
except i didn't give up, or at least i ain't tried to

i loved you.

i just didn't have enough for the both of us.

in my dreams, there is no fear
it's just you and me and how we used to feel

i wish i held onto you harder
i wish you held onto me in your darkness
i wish we both knew when to let go

we tried to fit into spaces we didn't belong
puzzles never finish with edges that don't look the same
they just fold and chafe into brokenness
until we bend in half

were you just not the one?
were we just too much?
will i look for your eyes in another man's gaze?

will it feel the same?

tracing lines

i woke up today feeling used and icky
this skin is itching to shed the remains of the touch you men have left on me
i'm tired
and i don't remember what love feels like
i just know i've searched for it in enough palms
tracing the lines and bruises that trickle your fingertips
they all lead to the same exit route
i've developed a sixth sense for knowing that the switch up is coming...
i'm about to be alone again.
i'm starting to blame myself.

honesty hour:

i don't know what it feels like to love just one person anymore.
so many people have had their hands in my chest.

it's not okay.

you are my muse.
but i swear to you,
this may not be a good thing.
my pain is not like cursive or calligraphy.
it is not pretty, and it is not poetic.
it is raw.
and shaky.
and rude.
unraveling these words feels like standing up too quickly.
waking up to sirens and not knowing what happened.
it is a rush of nausea and panic.
a slow fall into a place i do not want to visit.
it is a burden that blinds me.

i only write when i'm aching.
you have inspired a wave of it.
i know you don't think you did anything wrong.
in truth,
you didn't do anything i didn't do.
i just loved you more.
was willing to risk more.
fight more.
i love you more and this is my mistake.
so stop apologizing for the poems i write about you.
because i don't think i'm stoic enough to keep telling you it's okay..

dear _____:

i'm gonna pray for the girl you find me in.
i hope she's big enough to fill the shoes you took from me.

letters of a broken girl

if i allowed you to pick me a part, you would find my pieces in the hands of the men i loved. my father. my best friend. interlocked in the curls of the boy who taught me to hate myself. i am scattered and fluttering within the efforts of their new relationships. when she kisses him, she'll get a taste of the blood i bled for his evolution, and wonder who i am. he milked his way through me until my skin peeled. i tore myself apart. i hope it chokes her. i hope she drowns in my tears. i hope she goes to sleep with tremors in her chest, reminiscent of the nights i spent shaking out sobs. when she looks in the mirror, she'll see flashes of my reflection and wonder who she is to him. she'll smell peppermint and vanilla bean beneath his fingernails.
they have chunks of me still in their palms.
i made them into the men they chose to be for someone else.
i fought so they could love.
i don't have anything left.

how many times do i have to tell you?

1am shadows and sweaty bodies aren't substitutes for the truth you crave

you are tired of being alone.

these ecstasy-filled placeholders rinse sorrow from your voice
for a moment,

you can breathe again.

there is power in your skin,
this touch leaves men open mouthed and loose tongued

damn baby...don't stop.

yes girl, there is power in your touch
between your thighs
a power that drowns out loneliness
milks resolutions of celibacy to empty
until you forget why you ever gave this up

you are good at what you do,
and he loves it.
but it will not make him love you.

letting go is how i love you now

i am sure...

                                    that everyone i have ever been forced to let go of
                                            have scars trailing down their spines
                      guilty marks leftover from my clenched fingers and digging nails

                                                    i am not fond of moving on

                                                             or letting love go

              it takes me a while to realize how painful a grip i hold on to people
                                          when it's time to set them free
                                        it isn't until i look at my hands
                                              fingers torn and bloody
                                                      that i realize

                                                    my fear of being alone
                                                        has ruined me.

my condolences

what is evolution when growth feels like losing the best parts of you?
i've buried myself more times than i can count
i carry tombstones in my back pocket with all the quotes i used to believe in
plastered against the concrete slabs of who i used to be
i miss that girl
i miss believing in fairytales and longing for true love
i miss seeing the best in everyone, seeing my own reflection in the people i loved
i miss school girl crushes and the innocence of first kisses, and holding hands
i miss being who i was.
the girl who loved easily. and the girl who hoped. and the girl who didn't have to
worry about being strong all the time.
i don't want to be strong all the time.
i don't want to walk into rooms with my feet halfway out the door
i don't want to know what it feels like to triumph through pain
what is strength if it means being someone you've never wanted to be?
i've dug so deep inside of myself
pulling out the pieces of my soul that made me who i am
locking them beneath cellar doors
in an effort to be stronger
to protect myself
to hold my head high and become this manufactured superwoman that conquers
the world like life has taught me to be
but i didn't know that turning that key,
and digging those holes,
meant leaving myself behind.
i didn't know that it would make me unrecognizable.
resurrection impossible.
i don't know who i am anymore.
i don't know how to exist as me anymore.
i don't know what to do anymore.

something sweet

i think i'm addicted to heart break
i have lips that scream kiss me and a heart that falls in all the wrong directions
my hands like to touch all the wrong places
and there isn't really a time i can remember where i did not feel wounded
i'm not sure when or how crying shattered glass became second nature,
but i am tragically lost in hopeless love and lips that taste like marihuana
i inhale lost boys like it's the last drop of oxygen in helium chambers
and i float on the words of young men who will never be capable of truly loving me
but will spill enough passion to convince me to stay
and i convince myself
because being alone has never appealed to me
and sometimes it's easier to give myself away in exchange for something sweet to hold on to at night than it is to listen to the sound of my own pulse beating
'you deserve more'
some people dream of being rich
but i have always dreamed of being in love
so my heart has never been steady
and my feelings have never been calm
and i have been beaten and roughed up by this hunger to call somebody mines
for so long that these bruises seem permanently etched into my skin
i think i'm addicted to heartbreak
and this realization has left me scattered and afraid
i have never felt as wounded
as i am right now
sitting in my car crying fractured pieces of myself onto my steering wheel
i am broken.
i'm not sure when that word took up permanent residency inside my heart
or how it is even possible that my soul can so clearly resemble damage
but these feelings of inadequacy have taken root inside my throat
i have never so desperately wanted to divorce myself as much as i do now
because trying to piece together a puzzle without all the pieces is suffocating
i am a jigsaw of broken hearts and bookmarks
and everything else mixed in between the cracks of my soul feels foreign
i think i'm addicted to heartbreak
and i don't know how to quit.

how deeply loved i must have once been,
$\qquad\qquad$ to search for it again and again and again...

truth is...

there is one truth in this world i have come to accept as mostly absolute:
it will always be difficult to love another, without fully loving yourself.
there are some fleeting days, when i feel like Nubia
and this truth resonates deep inside my spirit
where i embrace that part of myself that leaps headfirst into pride carried like porcelain pearls
there are other days,
most days
where simply breathing is an accomplishment
because the journey of learning to love myself feels something like drowning
and i much rather jump to a place where there is someone to stay afloat with
where i don't have to travel oceans and paddle through hurricanes just to get to a land i've never seen.
there are some days, where i would like to think of myself as Nubia
all powerful and mighty
enormous in self determination
strong in spirit and adversary
but the fact is
i've never really been good at facing my fears
i am both selfish and gullible
i am more like an unfinished poem than something to take pride in
i am a cursed romantic and damsel in distress
there are some days, fleeting, where i feel like Nubia
there are some days, most, where i feel like me
and the thought of ever truly loving myself
seems too far away...

interludes

our relationship always felt like a rumor
a secret i always wanted to believe in
but
most stories like these are made up
i always had trouble remembering what came first when it came to us
did i love you because you loved me or did you want me because i loved
you or did i only confuse the rumors between our kisses for more than
what they really were,
the truth is…

**we only ever existed peacefully in quiet
and my love for you was too desperate to be pure**

your hands only touched mine in the shadows of movie theaters and
bedrooms that i mistakenly believed to be the interludes between a greater
connection,
in reality,

it was most of what we were.

you were never capable of telling me all your secrets
and i only told you mine because i thought it was what you wanted
i thought it would make you love me

and maybe you do
and maybe you always have
and maybe you always will

but you stuck a bookmark between my fingertips and told me to wait
and then you walked away
and you leaving taught me love does not conquer all
and relationships take more than just feelings

letting go is how i love you now

and the whispers between our connection will never be strong enough to heal these wounds

so i'm closing my ears.

and i'm closing my eyes

because we sound like a tragedy
and we look like a broken hourglass.
and i'm learning that time cannot heal all wounds if we continue to rip each other apart.

i love you and i hate you and i love you and i miss you and i want you and i love you and i love you i love you i love you i will never stop loving you i will always love you but

i'm out of breath.

so i'm picking my pieces off the ground
i'm cutting my fingertips on every kiss, and every conversation, and every smile shared between us,
i am caressing coconut oil onto these scars and bandaging all the wounds left from us
i am putting my life back together piece by piece
and remembering what it is like to heal myself.
i'm letting you go.
and it will take tears.
and it will take strength.
and it will take time
but i am learning that time....

time is all i need.

who are you still healing from?

letting go is how i love you now

letting go

(in my drowning, i see freedom. a chance to let go. the healing is in the releasing and the loving myself; again, and again, and again…)

letting go is how i love you now

rebirth

hurt still lives here

in the corners of my childhood bedroom

sleeping beneath my unconscious mind as it works to clear

to heal...

consider this your eviction notice

my mind is not an attic to hoard your fears

i am not this trauma and you are not my soul

this can't be your home anymore

come out from behind your hiding spots

i promise i'll hold your hand

i promise to point light into your darkness while i show you the way

so you can find God

so you can find You and be reborn...

note to myself, on doing the work-

i often feel silly chanting affirmations to myself
or praying
repeating things over and over
hoping that someday the words will melt into quiet whispers tattooed on my self-conscious until i truly believe them
i feel silly.
and i'm not sure how much of that is attributed to my lack of confidence, or lack of self-awareness.
i'm not sure how much of my discomfort comes from a place of masochism
or just disbelief.
i don't even necessarily think it's all of any of those things.
i don't think that i don't want to get better.
i want to be happy.
i want to experience self-love and self-worship
and i want to know what it's like to only need myself for once.
but i'm tired. and i'm broken.
and i do not want to do the work.
i do not want to repair something i didn't break alone.
sometimes it feels so unfair
that i must put so much effort into fixing myself
because of other people, and their clumsy fingers
i am tired of cutting myself on the shards you all created
what is the purpose of these hands if they're too bloody and too wounded and too raw to grasp anything
how do i put pieces back together when i'm still torn and shattered alongside them
how do i tell myself 'you're still worth loving'...when the wounds are still looking right at me

letting go is how i love you now

sugar glass

to the boy that i loved…

i wish i could heal you in all the places that you are hurting
like the ache in your palms from all the hearts you broke
and the tremor in your chest from all the women that suffocated you
i take some blame in your destruction.

yea you lied,
and yeah you damaged me,
and yeah you were selfish but—

i know our moments were real.

you once held me like sugar glass
and in all the years of our ups and downs
our climaxes and falters
our anger and joy
you held me like porcelain and i lost sight of that.

i knew you had slippery fingers
i knew your hands were unsteady when i chose to fall in love with you
i knew your feelings were as chaotic as my thoughts
as reckless as my hope
i knew i was easily broken before i ever let you touch me.
and for that, **i'm sorry.**

i am trying to dig deeper and deeper into myself,

into my flaws, and imperfections...

into my beauty and my strength...

i am pulling and grasping at the lining of my spine,

beneath my skin,

digging into my rib cage until i can no longer breathe his name,

touching my lips, clearing my throat and asking myself...

who are you?

transmutation

was all of she a façade?
as i peel back the layers of flesh i'm now made up of
there are parts of me i don't mind losing
there are parts of me i don't want to lose
will she be stripped raw?
will she be as interesting to you?
will i feel like myself again?
even in all this healing, it's still hard to imagine better than where she was.
will i get her back?
in all that fire and tenacity,
with this disconnection to revive,
will she be the same in my better?
is she still sane in the better?
is this really better?

dear _____:

i don't know if i should pray for you in this, or myself.

past life lover

there's another plane and another dimension
where we still exist
where loving you is easy and still right
where you pick me, as i pick you
and we write our future together in the same blue ink
harmoniously united
in a retrograde penmanship that has tied our souls for many realities
we're tied together now
even in our dissolution, there are reverberations of your soul still inside of me
lingering in the shadows of worry and missing
loving, and reflecting
chambers that carry your voice like you're right here, next door to my favorite place
somewhere
whispering my name in your own language
speaking to me in ways only you'll ever know how
we were special
we were pinky promises that i still don't view as broken
we tried our best
our love was, and is still, too great to not ever exist again
or somewhere else
it was too great to not ever exist at all
ever lasting
and ever reaching for golden sunsets
and all the moments where we felt right
we didn't last here
and that's okay
we were still glory, in our own little way
we were still good, even in the bad
we will have better, and still remember each other
during six am sunrises,
when we walk into our future kid's dorm rooms
or writing with chalk
we're eternalized on cardboard for life
written in future books
a story that you'll tell your grandchild one day...
we will have better
and i'll still miss you forever

venus

she has stars in her eyes the size of heart beats
shooting stars flashing by with the quickness of her own pulse
meteor showers of lost hope and heartache.
she's a display case of vulnerability
and honesty
a shadow of betrayal, and lies
she doesn't know she keeps asteroids lodged in her throat
destruction in her every breath
she is corrupted by passion
she's always had a habit of writing love stories out of tragedies
tearing out the pages where they both fall
only to narrate her on own crash in the end
she knows how to turn tranquility into chaos
she rash
and reckless
she manipulation and the manipulated
love has always been her sirens lullaby
her sailors call
and though her mind convinced her of its sinister illusions
her heart only sees it as magic.
she's always dreamed of being a recluse
to love only herself underneath constellations
her own magic, naked,
yet hidden.
but she is a dancer.
a lover.
a romantic.
a friend.
she craves body heat and infernos
voices
and fingers.
she lingers on ecstasy's touch
i love yous
and forevers.
she's more honest when her heart hurts
and doesn't completely understand happiness
but it doesn't matter.

letting go is how i love you now

she has a smile that lights up galaxies
and forgiveness that demolishes black holes
atlas himself cannot hold the weight of love she holds in her heart
and even aphrodite is jealous of her spirit.
this magic, this love
it's every mystical moment she craves
all the beauty she needs
love is her razor blade and ibuprofen
her dandelion and chicory flower
she has scars on her heart the size of goliath
but she still breathes constellations.
so the next time she says
i love you
name a star after yourself
and know that
she'll always be watching.

something to remember when the darkness visits you again:

sometimes the lights too bright
sometimes it feels better to rest in the shade
sometimes it's more healing to smile when no one can see

letting go is how i love you now

forever whole

*i have self-love quotes sprinkled across my skin
because i don't always have the capacity to believe i am enough
sometimes i forget.
so i trail my fingers across these tattoos in moments of weakness
in moments of being instinctively human
i remember the feel of valleys and dips alongside healed ink
i recite my quotes and whisper alone
i ink into my flesh
i touch myself, and i am reminded.
i am whole again.*

you feel battles on your shoulders like iron wrought hammers. you're an empath that can handle everyone else's emotions but her own. take a step back. remember the times when dreams were still thoughts and journeys seemed worth it. forget what ifs and if only. settle your heart. calm your anger and desperation for perfection. mountains exist. and potholes will always startle you. learn to slow and drive through them. even when you feel like crashing. even if your windshield cracks.

--because i am tired, exhausted, and discouraged today,
the things i must chant.
also, the things i must accept about myself
and the things i must change.

letting go is how i love you now

a eulogy

to all the men who didn't see the warmth in me
i pray your bed sheets don't always feel so empty
or so cold
they say if you dream about someone, it means they miss you
i hope you know it's a lie
i don't give a fuck.
when you lay awake ten minutes past 2am thinking of me
i hope you know that my days of crying
and trying
and wishing and missing ended once i realized that there is glory in me
there is God in me, even if you didn't see it,
i am made of porcelain and my cracks from being broken are filled with white gold
you may have destroyed me once upon a time but i stopped needing you
and then i stopped wanting you
and then i stopped missing you
and even though i may love you forever
i'll choose someone who feels the light
i'll choose someone who hears the heart
i'll choose someone who sees the mad in me and the dark in me and knows why it exist and doesn't fucking care
and i understand that it may mean being alone, it may mean choosing myself
because men are blind and men are selfish
and i've learned being in love with yourself is the next best thing to being in love with your child
i know what it's like to ache and love and love and hate at the same damn time
i pray the next girl makes you as happy as i tried to
i pray she has friends to cry to
i pray i always feel this strong.

notes to my future self:

just because someone is doing all the right things, it doesn't mean they're right for you.

learn to let things go, even if it scares you.

letting go is how i love you now

remembering

in my sleep, I am remembering

through pages of youthful memory

I watch over the shoulders of my past and remember

the who, the where, the why...

she calls my name in twilight hours

in the quiet, to make whole again

to let go of worry

to let go of fear, of pain

she places a hand on my chest and presses

as this energy bubbles over into my heart space

we labor my trauma

pulling muscles and pushing down,

my eyes turn inward and i'm hypnotized...

I see Heaven.

Between deep breaths, I remember

sweat forms droplets beneath my limbs

they hang heavy and I seep out of myself...

they rise tall and she remembers

I see her through these aches,

I hear her, and we remember

I breathe her into my fingertips and squeeze

beneath the pressure, there are always diamonds

waiting to be known

waiting to live outside and free

between light and breath

between life and death

tumbling out of my throat and into heaven

I open my mouth to speak.

I open my eyes

I see my heart

I see myself

*I wheeze in my name and exhale **God's**...*

letting go is how i love you now

something you mustn't ever forget:

shattered crystals still come from Heaven.
you will always be made of God.

An Ancestor's Prayer

You remind me of a woman I knew
all knocked kneed and free
all blue-belled and honey in every word she whispered
her voice dripped Venus when she spoke
She'd hopscotch her gaze in the darkest of corners and still see God
She looks just like You
brown buttered and french-kissed
her lips spoke vanilla
She smelled like lavender
She was frankincense and myrrh

You have her eyes
You see light, you see shadow
You see rogue in chocolate hues and still Love in all Your brokenness
her hands brand whole into Your collar bone

You been here before
Your wounds mend over in sage textured scars
You're made of Her healing

so, whenever You're ready,
just look in the mirror
when You've cried all that You can cry
and grieved Your aches and loss for lessons
pick Your chest up off the floor
unravel Your arms from around Our waist,
let Your insides out
unburden Our pain
open your eyes and fall back into Me...

letting go is how i love you now

letting go is how I love You now...

—Tiffany Aliyah

A Collection of Spoken Word Poetry

Performed and Written by Tiffany Aliyah Davis

www.ingramcontent.com/pod-product-compliance
Lightning Source LLC
Chambersburg PA
CBHW022020290426
44109CB00015B/1245